# IN DEFENCE OF ADULTERY

**Julia Copus** was born in 1969 in London, studied Latin at Durham University, and now lives in Blackburn. She won a Gregory Award in 1994. Her first collection *The Shuttered Eye* (Bloodaxe Books, 1995) was shortlisted for the Forward Prize for Best First Collection. In 2001, she received writing awards from the Arts Council of England and the Authors Foundation, and the following year was one of six writers in the North awarded a BBC/Gulbenkian Foundation writer's bursary. *In Defence of Adultery* (Bloodaxe Books, 2003) is her second book of poems. Both her collections are Poetry Book Society Recommendations.

# JULIA COPUS

# *In Defence of Adultery*

ERIC
BLOO
DAXE

## BLOODAXE BOOKS

ISBN: 1 85224 607 3

First published 2003 by
Bloodaxe Books Ltd,
Highgreen,
Tarset,
Northumberland NE48 1RP.

**www.bloodaxebooks.com**
For further information about Bloodaxe titles
please visit our website or write to
the above address for a catalogue.

Bloodaxe Books Ltd acknowledges
the financial assistance of Northern Arts.

Cover printing by J. Thomson Colour Printers Ltd, Glasgow.

Printed in Great Britain by
Cromwell Press Ltd, Trowbridge, Wiltshire.

*for W.J.R. Barber*

# Acknowledgements

Acknowledgements are due to the editors of the following publications, in which some of these poems first appeared: *Comic Verse* (Poetry Society, 1998), *London Magazine, Metre, Leviathan, New Blood* (Bloodaxe Books, 1999), *New Delta Review* (USA), *Oxford Magazine, Poetry Review, Staying Alive* (Bloodaxe Books, 2002), *Tabla, Thumbscrew, The Times Literary Supplement,* and *Writers' Awards 2001* (Arts Council of England). 'Freshwater Fish' won first prize in the 2001 Ilkley Literature Festival Poetry Competition.

I am also grateful for a Hawthornden Fellowship, and for grants from North West Arts Board, the Arts Council of England and the Society of Authors.

Special thanks to my father, and to Charlie, sine qua non...

# Contents

# I

# FISSION AND FUSION

'Would you tell me, please, which way I ought to go from here?'

'That depends a good deal on where you want to get to,' said the Cat.

'I don't much care where —' said Alice.

'Then it doesn't matter which way you go,' said the Cat.

LEWIS CARROLL, *Alice in Wonderland*


And if the world were black and white entirely
    And all the charts were plain
Instead of a mad weir of tigerish waters,
    A prism of delight and pain,
We might be surer where we wished to go
    Or again we might be merely
Bored but in brute reality there is no
    Road that is right entirely.

LOUIS MacNEICE, 'Entirely'

## Love, Like Water

Tumbling from some far-flung cloud
into your bathroom alone, to sleeve
a toe, five toes, a metatarsal arch,
it does its best to feign indifference
to the body, but will go on creeping
up to the neck till it's reading the skin
like braille, though you're certain it sees
under the surface of things and knows
the routes your nerves take as they branch
from the mind, which lately has been curling
in on itself like the spine of a dog
as it circles a patch of ground to sleep.
Now through the dappled window,
propped open slightly for the heat,
a light rain is composing
the lake it falls into, the way a lover's hand
composes the body it touches – Love,
like water! How it gives and gives,
wearing the deepest of grooves in our sides
and filling them up again, ever so gently
wounding us, making us whole.

# Cleave

## I

It was a cold winter that year, even in heaven.
The night your hearing gave up the ghost,
Lachesis had fallen asleep at her loom,
bruise-blue circles rimming her eyes.
The thread she had just been working
into the woof with chilblained fingers
broke and lay loose in her lap.
                                    And on earth,
from precisely that moment, your blocked-up ear
refused point-blank to swallow any more.
The mice in the attic over our bed
no longer stopped you from sleeping
and my scuffling feet on the flags
were quiet as dolls' by morning.
Within hours, your deafness had opened a gap
that stretched between us the length of the globe
till the soles of my feet, the soles of yours,
were planted in opposite quarters, cleaved
by 8,000 miles of rocks and seas
and we were north and south, antipodes.

## II

Or maybe that's not how it happened.
Let's say he settled his head on my lap
while I tilted a coffee-spoon of oil
warmed in a pan to the heat
of his skin and checked with a knuckle –
gingerly, gingerly – into the cave of his ear;
that on weighing the odds and taking stock
I was happy to stay for as long as it took –
so long, as things turned out, that my foot
became famed for the small patch of carpet, cleaved
to its sole, and the river we'd dreamed of living by
swam into view, and glittered through gaps
in the hawthorn tree. And spring began.

And as for the pool of oil
that had settled in his auricle
it must have been a libation,
for the gods in time returned to him
first the sensation of traffic –
buses that chanced it up Limbrick
making the living-room windows shudder;
a little while later, the tick of my watch;
my stockings shifting under my skirt;
and finally, far off, a goddess waking
next to her loom, the crack
of her fingers taking up the slack.

# Essence

It's the way a simple olive might exude
the story of a narrow coastal road
that climbs the mountains under the Mistral
through aisles of cypresses, a scorching sun;

how on certain nights, late on in winter,
the surface of the ocean shrinks to a fog,
eclipsing tiny harbours and their clutch
of scruffy, icicle-fringed fishing boats.

I want the epigram, not the epic,
the Guiding Principles, the Rule of Three,
the shift of continents and rise of nations
summed up in an inky paragraph.

I want it all cut short, the gist, in a nutshell,
to come direct to this – beyond the nights
of brooding underneath each other's windows,
beyond the weight, the sleep, the face we've lost –

this leaning in, this six-inch square of table
in which your hand lies, telling me you want me.

## Love Scene

Wait – we want to get this in the can –
the light, the temperature, the shadow-scatter
blown just so from the trees. We want it all,
from the moment your Cartesian cogito
starts feeling kind of blurred round the edges;
the moment you catch sight of him. That's good.
And close-up now: sun-chiselled shadows moving
on his lips, the pages of his book...
Cut to interior. If only you could see
what we can: something like a shadow
opening its feathery-soft wings
inside you. This is beautiful.
Go with it. No, don't even think about
resisting. Feel it – like a wound
you hug to you, like someone in the grip
of madness, rocking her body for comfort.
And stand by: it's any minute
*now*. We pick that up? – That flip
into tachycardia? That's really something,
isn't it? Let's zoom
a little closer in on what she's seeing here:
the hive of her body swarming
under his hands. Just keep them rolling.
This is something else.

# Oubliette

## I *Wedding Nerves*

It is night in the town, blue-black and chill
where a line of punts lies tethered, nosing
at the boathouse wall. Close by here a man,
who isn't quite my father yet, is pacing
back and forth along the river-path.
Tall branches make a larynx for the wind.
My father has no voice tonight, but look:
his hair is lit like words as if the moon
has lifted it the way it lifts the river.
*The world is turning imperceptibly,*
he seems to say, *and if I add to this –*
*if I add the quickness of my steps,*
*how fast, then, am I moving and how soon*
*will it be morning?*
                        And now he stops, mid-
thought, mid-path, remembering the cold
holiness of that winter church, the banns
read out and how he flushed and knew the growth
that itches from a root in early spring
and blazes in the bud and anything
seemed possible, in reach, and was.
                                    Tomorrow
he will be husband like the tallest tree.

Elsewhere, at this hour, lips will be planting
kisses and blessings on their children's heads,
over which freshly-washed vests will go
in the twilit dusk, little heads and hands
pushing into neck-holes and arm-holes – *arms
up to heaven.* Now it is lights out,
the streets are all empty – acres of cold roofs...
But here, in a three-bed semi on the edge
of town, the children's rooms are empty now.
Here's a candle, with its blue flame blooming
and wilting on the stem. And here
is my father, who is my father now.
If the label's genuine, his Laphroaig
was shut in its cask when he was married.
This, tonight, would be his crystal year:
he tips his glass again and takes the light
liquor on his tongue, the glassy dome
decanting to the mouth-dome. He is all fire –
*This home is not my home, though it belongs
to me. I have children. I said to them:
'I am the tree of knowledge, you my branches.'
Their silence told me that they understood;
their tiny hands, their nails... Our bough was strong,
but she was stronger, like the wind that frets
at the cradle's hinges, the treetop's limbs.*

### III  *Second Home*

Where the long hall ended the living-room
began. What I mean is, I don't remember
a door before then. Today there's a door
and it's shut. My Daddy's visiting.
I dressed by firelight and nobody heard,
I did it so quietly. Now I'm outside:
a snowy landscape and a blur of red.
It's school-time and I'm in my wellingtons,
trying to stamp a path along the drive.
This time I make it to the dustbin, half
sunk in snow, when my heels skid and the sky
leaps over my head like that and smack...
This noiselessness, is it the sky or me?
When he got here it was in the night –
too late for me, yes, but he should have come
to wake me anyway. I would have liked it.
I tread back through my footprints, past the room
where he's asleep now and I want to peep
inside it but the curtains are shut tight,
and sounds of school are trickling down like poison
from the far end of the street. I edge
my way along the side-wall to a door
which opens and my mother's standing there.
I've tried three times to make it to the end
and now I'm crying, telling her I can't
do it – *please* – I want Daddy to take me.

IV  *Dead Dad*

It's spring at last – a thousand tiny birds
cascading from the blue cloak of the sky.
The shadows are clean-cut, the cool sun split
wide open on the pavement into light
and dark. My father knew a trick like that.
He'd step inside the cupboard murmuring
*Now I shall lie down in the grave; seek me*
*and I shall not be.* And when he left for real
we thought of him appearing somewhere else,
walking off stage, bowing *Thank you, thank you.*
He hadn't gone for good, but in the end,
you understand, we tired of his vanishings.
We let them peel away from us like skins.

# Hymn to All the Men I'll Never Love

My heart, sing praises to the men
I'll never love; from whom a night
away's just that – a night – and not
a lifetime in the desert without food
and water. It's because of them
that breakfasts can be eaten, Lord, appointments
kept, and letters left to lie
where they have fallen; men with whom
a perfect evening may be nothing more
than beer and cards outside beneath the lean-to
where straight-talk and easy gestures leave
dark nests of sparrows and the scent
of bonfires in their wake; the sort of men
whose smiles I can endure without
surrendering my all to them;
in whose unswerving disregard,
let heaven rejoice, let the earth be glad.

# Home Physics

**Mechanics:** standard pan balance with assorted weights; film loop: *Flea and Dry Ice Puck* (sound, 5 mins); card snapped from under a weight by a leaf spring; tablecloth yanked out from under dishes; bowling ball pendulum swings back to nose; sledge hammer hits large mass resting on person; train on circular track moves one way and track moves the other. **Fission and Fusion:** mousetrap chain reaction. **Waves:** rubber rope stretched across front of room; film loop: *Tacoma Bridge Collapse* (silent, 4 mins); tuning forks, various; one tuning fork with tuned cavity drives another; giant tuning fork, barely audible, displayed with stroboscope; standing sound waves in flames along a large pipe; ball bounces off end of stroked rod. **Heat and Matter:** dry cleaner bag rises to ceiling; wire sieve boat floats on water until alcohol is added; film loop: *Irreversibility and Fluctuations* (silent, 7 mins). **Optics:** standard colour blindness tests, box of coloured yarns; phantom bouquet: real image from a concave mirror; horn thermopile and mirror sense candle across room. **Astronomy and Perception:** vault of the heavens: large lucite globe.

# Lamb's Electronic Antibiotic

Just as a holy man will turn aside
to pray, reflect, and be still before God,
when Lamb's life went from bad to worse he took
to coming here. The low roof hung hood-like
over his head. It seemed to be as good
a place as any for the job, this shed,
this backyard makeshift workshop, calm with books
and instruments: a lamp, a UV box
with a loose lid, from which a blue light curled.
Bit by bit he came to know the world
of scheming and invention and things born
bewildered, in the watery light of dawn.
He kept a stash of 10-year-old Laphroaig
beside him as he went, pouring a slug
into a glass to sip, and teased his dreams
from formless fibres into diagrams
of circuits that would govern a machine
for wiping out diseases of the skin.
His eyes shone: *Under a stream of charged air,*
he reasoned, *every canker, wound and sore*
*will shrivel back to nothing, retrograde.*
Now his project gathered to a head.
Now anything seemed almost possible –
*Even the rifts that form between people*
*are easily spanned*, he thought, *after the rot*
*is stopped, scraped back, and as often as not*
*a bridge can be re-grown across a gap –*
and in this way he kept from giving up.
At last he held a fledgling prototype
beneath the glow of the oscilloscope,
a photoplotted maze of paths and gates
like plans for a whole new town, with parks and streets
and one-way systems fixed on acetate,
a place so real he might inhabit it...
With pink-gloved hands under the window's hush
he rocked the coated circuit in a dish
until the details swam back into view,
the blue resist uncoiling, breaking free.

The shed was like a ship's cabin that night,
a submarine that cruised beneath the light
of morning where he dreamed his life restored –
the little upturned dinghy in the yard
purged of its woodlice and afloat again
on clear waters under a cloudless sun.
He saw the weeds that poked up through the gaps
between the flags retreat like periscopes,
the moss clumps loosen from the greying thatch,
and in his mind he scaled the house to watch
moss-capsules sealing round their spores, rhizoids
detaching till the thatch's flaky reeds
sprang back to glossy ovate tubes. He planned
to bring the gardens, everything he owned,
back to the newness of that golden roof;
and then to stand beneath it with his wife,
the dark patches of hurt on both their hearts
dissolved away, betrayals and retorts
erased at last, each by the other's side,
the air between them stable, purified.

## Widower

I believe it was a calm evening,
when the sky was least expecting it,

the volcano snapped awake and oozed
a country, which darkened, hardened, formed

per second per second through the years
to shape the landscape we scrambled through

our last summer together, searching
for the dusty chapels underground,

paintings of Christ with the eyes scratched out.
She looked so small beneath them even then,

her first time abroad. Soon after, the earth
reached up and kissed her, full on the mouth.

And now I'm back in this tea-garden
we visited – city of two

continents, they call it – I like that,
the cool water running in between.

I like the honesty of the place,
the way it speaks of uncertainty,

like these first stars twitching at the brim
of the parasol. Even the sea

can't stop its lip from trembling at the shore.

# Hearsay

Again, the kettle's rhetoric: click,
b-r-e-a-t-h-e... It has a hidden lung
of unimaginable dimension.

I have left the blind down, darling, on our sky-
light, night-blue, and all day
the answer-phone's a mouthpiece
for double-talk and subterfuge.
The fax is planning to publish
a play for voices under its own name.

And on our long oak table
a diary which predates me
holds parts of your life with people
I never knew: *ribs, breasts, lips, hair* –
these are what you loved once
about a particular girl and no girl
in particular: *your voice, your silly voice.*

# Breaking the Rule

## I *The Art of Illumination*

At times it is a good life, with the evening sun
gilding the abbey tower, the cold brook

sliding past and every hour in my Book
a blank page, vellum pumiced

to a lustre, so the inks won't spread –
saffron and sandarach and dragon's blood,

azure and verdigris. Monsters and every type of beast
curl round the words. Each man here has a past,

and each man reasons for his faith.
I wronged a woman once.

My floor is strewn with thyme and rosemary
to mask the odours – fish glue, resins

vinegar and oils. With these I draw
the hosts of the redeemed, and every face

takes on the features of a face I've known
and every angel's face beneath the shadow

of its many-coloured wings is hers alone.

## II *The Art of Signing*

There are ways among the stone and shadow
to transgress the Rule. We speak

in signs: a language with no grammar.
For the sign of bread you make a circle

with your thumbs and index fingers – like the belt
that pressed the silk against her waist.

For an eel, you place one fist on top of another,
as if grasping a cord of hair to kiss

that one mouth only in the frantic din
of the ale-house, where we used to dance,

and later outside in the grainy dusk
our four feet shuffling over the quiet earth.

For the sign of silence put a finger
to the dry muscle of your mouth,

the darkness that's inside it. Keep it there.

## Freshwater Fish

In the deep night, alone now, with the house
drifting eastwards she recalls his eyelashes

scratching her neck like wings, his fidgety
woodland eyes, the nights he'd dreamed himself

a boy again, broken by the hack of his father's cough
and the barked command, blood-gargled – *Bucket!* –

which, even in his sleep, he swore he could find,
fetch and hold to his father's chin in under a minute.

She thinks, *Wherever you are, be here; I want*
*to carry your absence in me like a sleepy sea-*

*animal. A wound.* Her hair is bound
with lengths of coastline they journeyed to –

waterfalls, rock-pools, hot tracts of sky.
Sometimes she asks out loud, *Where did you go*

*with your fisherman's jumper wrapped round you*
*like a landscape?* He comes back to her then –

sometimes, at night, he comes – in his green
waders from the edge of the water, clanking

buckets of pink lungs, bright as freshwater fish.

# Leaving

It was for fear we'd sleep too long
and wake to find the frail shapes of children
grown from us like limbs.

My heart had walked those unknown streets
in spite of me, holding out its doll-like hands
for nourishment, for more.

# Playing It By Ear

## *Threshold of Audibility* (0 dB)

This is what she'll tell them afterwards:
that given the diffidence of the soundscape –
hoof-steps, leaf-flutter,
the ancient forest crackling with rain –
that coaxed the first
incipient, coiled-up nub
of inner ear to bud, to form a drum
and to extend towards the troposphere
three ossicles, like tentacles, to hear,
she would have thought the words that fell from her
night after night, like tiny desperate bombs,
might trigger some response – or failing that
a flame held to the edge of his evening paper.

What happens next will be out of her hands,
for what he seems to hear's precisely nothing:
nothing moves or speaks except the flames
that reach up like an alleluia chorus
over the World in Brief and keep on reaching,
while the shabby armchair grafted to his thighs,
that's spent its shabby armchair-lifetime dreaming
of how to fly, uplifts light as a skiff
into the space the roof has opened for it –
and hovers there with its unwitting pilot.
His dark hair, ringed with effervescing light,
drinks in information from the air:
reports, statistics, rumours, fairy-tales
like the one about the wife who, pushed to her limit,
apparently did X and then did Y.

### Quiet Garden, Whispered Conversation (30 dB)

All the while, between the apple branches,
she keeps in sight her daughter's golden head,
the white and pale pink deckchair-stripes that frame it,
and speaks in a whisper, anxious not to wake her.
For she is fast asleep, a sleep as fast
as the hard tight buds of winter aconites
pushing through their green sheaths on the lawn.
Sanders has come to fix the garden gate.
*It'll need a whole new sneck, will that*, he says,
and shakes his head at where her husband has
cobbled something together from string and a nail.
*Useless*, she whispers, and tugs at the makeshift latch.
But when she feels his warm hand close round her hand
she holds her breath and keeps her blue eyes lowered
on the patch of rust that has come off on her fingers,
the gold of her daughter's hair, the luminous clouds
hosting and breaking in her coffee cup.
*Useless*, she whispers again, and the mauve of her eyelids
covers her eyes, like petals, or shells; *a dead loss.*

## Moderate Restaurant Clatter (50 dB)

Half way through the main course when her husband
is chewing grimly on a plate
of sole grand succès she suppresses an urge
to scream at him *Call this a life?*
*You, of all people, who gave me my own life,*
*back then – that first morning – when love set about*
*stitching a sail to my heart. Let me tell you,*
*my eyes went out into the world that day,*
*blotting up cityscapes, sunsets, cathedrals...*
But the night is uncomfortably warm, and the air
is crawling with smiles and earrings and necks,
and she thinks of the way those insatiable necks
would turn, one by one, and the glugging of wine
and the wavering candle flames, how they would stop,
stock-still on their stiff little stems.
                                          And so
the moment passes as such moments do.
*At least*, she thinks, *we still have this between us*
(the bowls of their wineglasses brimming like rock pools).
But there, at the window, something is waiting:
a presence – like water – but wild, like a river
that stretches from here to beyond and forever.
And in her mind she lays down her silver
and takes up his hand and makes him go with her,
leaving themselves, who don't know any better,
to the necks and the smiles and the half-eaten dinner,
the interminable, moderate restaurant clatter.

The first time they spoke
away from each other
and he from respect –
just a train ride away
for a while on the opposite
their small voices carrying,
He chipped at a weed
and they talked of the weather,
boom in the markets,
how it rose or fell,

they were standing a metre
– she out of shyness
on a street, in a town
from a place they would own
side of the river,
loud in the heat.
with the tip of his shoe
perhaps, or the imminent
the price of oil,
according to this or to that.

And of course at the time
the haziest notion
they'd hold with that distance
or indignant, exhausted,
occur to them then
how a space of that size
Things tumbled into it
over the years,
the papers he'd pore over,
the restaurant tables
eyes would meet
their fair-headed daughter

neither one of them had
of other discussions
between them – aloof,
despondent. It didn't
– and why should it? – to think
might be filled. They grew old.
more or less randomly
whatever would fit –
corner to corner;
across which their hesitant
or not; or the height
would grow to one spring.

If they'd paused then to think,
and weighed up their chances
but she wanted the gap
she longed for her ear
till the sound of his voice
but felt, in her skull,
her cranial vault.
if he lowered his eyes
of her cotton-print dress
made it flutter so lightly,
Or that when he looked up
had settled in patches
so by then there was no
they might have proceeded
towards the forever,

if they'd thought at the start,
or drawn up a list...
to be closed, and they both did;
to be flush to his chest
was no longer heard
in the length of her jawbone,
And was it his fault
from her eyes to the hem
when he did, if the breeze
just then, on her legs?
it was late and the sunlight
the length of the street
time to lose? If there had been
more slowly, with caution,
towards the forever.

## Empty Shoes

Through this floating wall the telephone
is sulking like a needy child, demented
with longing. It's remembering
the thrill of your voice along its wires,
and might cry out at any moment.

My shoes are out there somewhere too –
stiff-jointed, restless. One of them
is under the illusion I'm a princess;
I could open the window now and let it
make its way to you, go clopping down
the night-filled roads to give you the idea
that I am lost and that you'd like to find me.

# Glimpses of Caribou

It's their placid manner
that surprises us
when at the edge
of our vision we glimpse them,
ambling aimlessly
over the paths of the choices we make,
rooting in hummocks of sedge.
And there's something we love
in that way they have
of travelling for travel's sake.
Somehow it comforts us
to look up from the cusp
of an irksome decision,
a fork in the road, and see them –
the shape of an antler,
the gleam of a coat.
*Which way do we go?*
we say to the baffled caribou
who from a long way off
look back at us, and then
are gone – into a landscape
glistening with lakes;
on expandable feet
on hard-packed snow:
a clicking of caribou
tendons and hooves
cutting a trail in the rock
which future caribou,
chancing on it,
may choose to follow, or not.

# II

# ASTRONOMY AND PERCEPTION

Two men looked out from prison bars;
one saw mud, the other stars.

ANONYMOUS

Observations reveal that vast halos of invisible matter
surround galaxies and galaxy clusters. The inflationary
theory, if true, demands that this dark stuff makes up
between 90 and 99 percent of the universe.

STEPHEN HAWKING

# In Defence of Adultery

We don't fall in love: it rises through us
the way that certain music does –
whether a symphony or ballad –
and it is sepia-coloured,
like spilt tea that inches up
the tiny tube-like gaps inside
a cube of sugar lying by a cup.
Yes, love's like that: just when we least
needed or expected it
a part of us dips into it
by chance or mishap and it seeps
through our capillaries, it clings
inside the chambers of the heart.
We're victims, we say: mere vessels,
drinking the vanilla scent
of this one's skin, the lustre
of another's eyes so skilfully
darkened with bistre. And whatever
damage might result we're not
to blame for it: love is an autocrat
and won't be disobeyed.
Sometimes we manage
to convince ourselves of that.

# Comet

Mid-March the spectroscopes discovered it,
the strength of its light curve, its integral flux,
triggering months of frenzied speculation:

if it landed in the ocean, how the ocean –
teeming with jellyfish, sailing boats, pieces of shingle –
would come to the people for once, and flatten the gates

of their churches and schools, tear down their offices, law-courts,
cinemas, playgrounds and stadiums, leaving behind
glistening plateaux of mud where cities once stood;

or if it hit the land, how dust from the crater
would spread through the sky and form a cloud so vast
that the sun would be darkened for days, for weeks perhaps.

As late as May, the night sky bore a faint
stain like a rainbow – cobalt, violet, madder –
colours which a night photographer

would fix that month, and afterwards explain
as particles of sunlight in the dust tail
that streamed from the shimmering head of the comet.

But in the kitchen of her tiny flat,
my aunt, bowed at the sink, sees none of this.
A spinster, beautiful at thirty,

she's shelling beans, pushing her thumb again
and again into the silky inner sac
and watching as they gather in the base

of a bakelite dish, like tiny speckled planets.
Later, her golden head bent over the wash-bowl,
and a heel of white moon showing at the window,

she'll lift the tea-plates out of the dirtying water
and it's only then that the vestiges of comet
will peter out into the dark at the rim of the earth.

All of which takes place to illustrate
how little or how much exists between
the drift of what is and what might have been;

how, in the single act of looking up,
from the brim of a hat, from a plate or a book,
our lives may be changed for good – witness, my aunt:

this morning, in the market-place, a man
strode by her, kicking up a cloud of dust
in which it was just possible to see

a ghostly entourage of wedding guests,
a flimsy white sheet from the marriage bed
contorting in the breeze and, further back,

a string of golden-haired children in tow,
but she was kneeling then, to tie her shoe.

# Atrophy

Why, when we refuse to be drawn
or even to listen, choosing instead to sit
by ourselves, in the dark, at the edge
of the open floor, are we surprised
to find at length our purplish hearts
have stiffened and our limbs that once
gleamed with infinite possible gestures
– foxtrot, quickstep, pas de deux –
have set themselves into the narrow shape
of our chores, like late-night caretakers
who find themselves, after the music's gone,
walking behind their baffled brooms
stiffly, left, right, left, through emptied halls?

## Topsell's Beasts

Who can say for certain that such creatures
don't exist – sea-wolves and unicorns,
and lamias with their *exemptile eyes*
which they can lever out and lay aside
for rest after a kill? Why can't we believe,
as people like us used to believe,
that lemmings graze in clouds,
that apes are terrified of snails,
that elephants grow meek and timid when they see
a lovely girl, that mice may be spontaneously
*ingendered in the earth*, weasels give birth
through tunnels in their ears, or reindeers
when they walk make noises like
the sound of cracking nuts? So much
of what we know we take on trust.
Trust, then, that though you find me 'hard to handle',
on long late days full to the lintel
with love like this, I may be calm and gentle –
pliant, even, like the camelopardal
with his fifteen-foot long neck diversely coloured
and *so easie to be handled that a child
may lead him with a line of cord, homeward.*

# A Short History of Desire

On a day like today, I think I can almost
begin to make sense of those chivalrous knights
who, on the whim of some titian-haired damsel,
would set off on horseback, although they were barely
out of their teens, in pursuit of some noble
improbable task, while a sun much like this one
strobed through the trees and the left-behind girl
perfected the art of the meaningful wait –
the curve of her breasts and her full lips so pleasingly
matching the line of the coiled anaconda
thickly entwined like a creeper about
her chiffon-swathed hips, the nub of its head
reclining over her naked shoulder.

As naked, that is, as the thigh of the fabled
Victorian gent (beneath the folds
of his peg-top pants) who, perched on a horsehair
chair in the parlour, would catch a glimpse
of his lady-love's finely-turned ankle and feel
the strain of his flesh at the seam of his button-up
fly; was suddenly, keenly, aware
of the fervour of light, how it filled up a room
on a day like today, how it tugged at his blood,
and glanced off the edge of her silver-plate buckle

the way in the Fifties it glanced off the fenders
of a thousand parked-up Morris Minors
under the moon when the sweetest of girls
might take off her clothes on a day like today
to the radio's chanting – *alop-bam-boom* –
and lie back like a leaf-bud splitting
open across someone's trembling lap as if
just then a knife had been touched to her skin.

However deep asleep you think you are,
there always will be days like this –
a light, hair-tousling breeze and a sun that streams
into the dusty parlour of your heart.

Pray when it does that your heart, out cold
for the winter, stirs in its stockpile of leaves.
Or else, that you're caught off guard by the quickening
thump of your hoof-beat heart returning
from very far off: pray then for the stoutness of heart
to ride with it headlong into a poem like this one
where some part of everything never stops moving
under the light of that big old heart, the moon;
where even the moon up there in its ocean
of sky is afloat, and trembles with longing.

# Loch

Remember that night, flint-dark with the rain
chipped in it, lamplit? Cut to our feet
black boot-shelled shifting tarmac, kerb,
whole skeins of tenemented streets,
into the history starting to form
in the silence at our backs. Look up:
a loch had approached us, overlapped
with noctilucent cloud and stopped
just short, at the edge of us. *What's all that
white stuff?* I asked – and it was swans
drifting out from under a mountain.
And shapes of the mountain on the dark
surface of the loch drew back
as the swans came closer and the water
broke and sealed to let them enter
our heads for just as long, no longer,
than a trick of the light could manage to gather
black loch, white swans and us, together.

## Possibility

Some days feel a budding in their stems,
an itch in the skin of things:
walls soften; a chair becomes lissom,
acquiring a suppleness in its frame;
a book, straight-backed and serious,
takes to the air; and the carpet
shifts and loosens on its sea-bed.
On such days it is down to us
whether we wait for things to pass
or manage, with a simple gesture,
to inslide ourselves, cut loose, set sail –
vessels of the possible.

## Radio SFX

The intimacy of the bar –
low sofa, *sotto voce*,
lights down low –
is really an unfurnished studio.
And what you take to be
a crackling fire
is only a square
of cellophane
that someone's twisting near
the microphone.
All well and good –
it can go ahead
without so much
as the blink
of a blinked eyelid.
For when what happens next
happens 'outside',
it's a flat dry space
with, in it, footfalls, crunched
from a box of starch
to represent the snow
laid out from here
to the quiet branch-line railway
he'll walk her to,
*en route* to which,
*en passant*, it will happen –
the bit we've all of us
been waiting for –
where one of the lovers'
mouths makes contact with
the other lover's mouth –
they kiss, press bodies,
and are near as dammit making out
beneath those railway arches
and it's fine,
it's quite all right,
for his arm to be squeezed in
up to the elbow almost
in the waistband

of her skirt like that – what is this,
after all? It is only
a man and a woman
in a dead room somewhere,
sucking the backs of their hands.
So why is it I envy them?
– that easy way they have
of walking back
along a labyrinth
of corridors to where,
parked in adjoining bays, their cars
have given up their colours
to the dark.
He takes the exit north,
and she goes south.
And, when you think of it,
it stands to reason.

# Soft Parts

*Paleontologists treasure the rare geological circumstances*
*that permit an occasional preservation of soft parts.*
STEPHEN JAY GOULD

Perhaps there is some transcendental place,
some cove or lair,
somewhere in which
the pouches, lobes and gills,
suckers, lips and tentacles
of countless ancient animals
endure. For bones are not much more
than relics, really.
A carpal or talus –
what can it tell us
of the monk-seal's passion
for sunbathing on sandbars,
the muntjac deer's
fondness for tea-leaved willow?
So little of a fellow
can be surmised
when all that was supple
has gone from a creature.
You see this with people
of a certain nature: even in life
the softness of their mouths,
their eyes and hearts
stiffen and harden
till nothing remains
to show us what they were,
that they were human.

# Regret

There could be a madman or a harpy
in that hard-shelled seed you buried recently,
thinking *It is limbless, what harm can possibly
come of it?* Alone now in the soft-soiled grainy
dark it's using all its balled-up energy
to split the husk, push out a tiny gristly
root... Oh, you can't hear it, but already
it's making headway, nudging a pasty-
looking stem towards the light, an airy
space it will bloom into, carefully
cut for it out of the indigo sky. What a panoply
of stories it will tell when it bristles with willowy
arms and legs of its own! You had better be wary,
for years later when your dinner-party
guests are stepping inside from the shiny
moonlight-lacquered pavements of whatever city
you have moved to, when the wine is quietly
breathing in its jug, the nickel-plated cutlery
is silent and anxious, going over its clattery
small-talk on the table – that's when your heavy-
hearted monster leans his bulk, very gently,
over your house, puts his mouth to your chimney
and with a kind of funnelled clarity
addresses you.

## Out

It seemed the obvious place to go, the sea.
And when he reached it there it was, exactly
as he had remembered it; it didn't pause
or lift its gaze but went on casually
sporting at the land's edge,
kitted out in the usual ships and birds.
*I am no one*, said the cricketer;
*my playing days are done.* And he lay down
flatly as a wave in the shade of a cove
and filled up his ears with the sound of the wind
to muffle the beating of his conscious mind.
And when he next looked up again
a mesh of rain had occupied the sky.
The ships had left the harbour and the birds were gone.
Only the waves remained: dumb, emphatic,
arching and falling in the fibrous light, just
arching and falling into themselves
the way a ball describes itself in flight.

# Deskscape

The surface is all cracks, like the parched
mud of a river-bed with its silt
of skin flakes and old thoughts.
In the dark of the window a sixty-watt bulb
shines like a saint from its metal hood.

Close to my bent head the lamp
cranes its rubber neck, intent
on catching the words it speculates
will fall soon helter-skelter with the dust,
the way a schoolboy waits for ants to come
scuttling into a circle of lit earth
beneath his magnifying glass.
And so I keep them, tucked
in the sleeve of my mouth.

The flowers lean in, too, craving attention.
I push my thumbnail into them and their
plump flesh darkens and weeps round the little wound.
And now they will go on weeping into the night,
weeping and breathing loudly in their fat jug.

Without me, this whole house
would exist quite happily: the staircase would go on
guiding the carpet up to the same room, the exact same
desk with its bleak geography, its saintly presence.

# Kim's Clothes

*(for my cousin, Kim, 1958-1997)*


The summer you died and your mother sent me your clothes,
that was a fitful time: whole streets were possessed
by a wild wind, quick-fingered, able
to pick a roof to its bones; trees were upturned.
One night, just to the north of here, it managed
to drive a freight ship inland with its hammering,
wind-racked cacophony. A hellish storm, it was.
And for weeks, cousin, each long day shrank to a strange,
sobering sight: your clothes pooled on the floor.
For weeks I slept, woke, slept, but always returned to that same
thought – how the things she did back then would matter later.
I thought it must have helped to tend to them,
these clothes she laundered and stacked, her heart gone cold
like the rooms she moved through, bending, gathering,
her head quiet as a storm-wrecked sea,
the iron sailing through the dark inside,
as if it wasn't you but she who'd died.
Grief-gagged, grief-girt, she went about her work
thinking perhaps I might make use of them,
holding them up to the light, the soft tubes of their arms.

Holding them up to the light, the soft tubes of their arms,
thinking perhaps I might make use of them,
grief-gagged, grief-girt, she went about her work
as if it wasn't you but she who'd died,
the iron sailing through the dark inside
her head – quiet as a storm-wrecked sea,
like the rooms she moved through, bending, gathering
these clothes she laundered and stacked, her heart gone cold.
I thought it must have helped to tend to them,
thought how the things she did back then would matter later.
For weeks I slept, woke, slept, but always returned to that same
sobering sight: your clothes pooled on the floor.
And for weeks, cousin, each long day shrank to a strange,
wind-racked cacophony. A hellish storm, it was,
to drive a freight ship inland with its hammering.

One night, just to the north of here, it managed
to pick a roof to its bones; trees were upturned
by a wild wind, quick-fingered, able.
That was a fitful time – whole streets were possessed –
the summer you died and your mother sent me your clothes.

# Portrait of My Neighbour Skipping

To judge by the way her body tenses
into the jump, it's as if she believes

that the ills of the world are stranded and bound
in the skipping ropes of little girls –

like this one she keeps at arms' length with the sky
heaped on its back. It's as if she senses

she'd hear, if she put the rope to her ear,
the wickerwork creaking of families breaking,

the static of voices that worms through the carpets
at night in the bedrooms of other girls' houses;

that flows through the skirting boards into our gardens,
and shorts at the rubberwood handles she's gripping.

The way she loops herself there in an arc
and picks up her delicate feet to the rhythmic

snap of the rope explains she is learning
to take things in her stride, and it shows

how different she is from me, whose feet,
at eight, are already too big to negotiate

the cracks in the pavings along our street
under which – listen – a sleuth of bears

is gathering, rumbling out of their lairs
to the snap, like ropes, of their cavernous jaws.

# Forgiveness

Even the most delicate
cut-crystal champagne flutes
can mop up 90 decibels
with very little visible
effect (their placid throats
remain intact), but if a note's
played steadily, and at the proper
frequency, sooner or later
they will shatter. Those with a lower
lead content last longer.
And so with us: some of us buckle
under the smallest
slight, while others acquire
a lustre, like the sheer
gleam of a pearl,
as if something that's valuable
and rare is grown from the gritty
onslaughts they endure.
Perhaps it's just
that what they ask of us
is more realistic – maybe this
alone has made their hearts
more pliable than ours,
more elastic.

# Esprit de l'Escalier

There's bits of sticky underlay
beneath my nails, splinters and carpet fluff
lodged in my hair – it's close-up work
requiring surgeon-like precision to maintain
the saw-blade at exactly the angle I need
to lift one neat-edged slice of stair
but leave the words intact, nestling like eggs
I'll scoop out and slip carefully into my pockets.

And this is what I have in mind
for afterwards: a scarlet-sequinned dress,
a sweeping staircase to descend
with you at the top of it watching the sway
of my neat little red-spangled arse getting
smaller and smaller, the words that I'll throw at you,
stomping their way up the steps of your heart,
slamming the door shut and settling there, growing
harder, ounce by ounce, like wet cement.

## Chicken-script

I have put them all in cages –
lovers, houses, landscapes –
penned in by loops
of wiry chicken-script.
And now I'm free
to come and go from them.
The past is a vivarium
with a ticket on the fence
of each exhibit: *spouses*
*weighing up the odds;*
*lovers at the limit*
*of their self-control;*
*villain on the cusp*
*of coming good.*
For now it holds
though this
like any other fence
is at the mercy
of the elements.

# NOTES

**Home Physics** (23): The titles here are taken from a list of demonstrations used in physics lectures at the University of California.

**Lamb's Electronic Antibiotic** (24-25): In 1991 my father invented a machine called the Biogun, which was marketed as 'the world's first electronic antibiotic'. The machine has a wand which, when pointed at an infected surface, produces a concentrated stream of electrically-charged air particles which kill the microbes causing the infection.

**Playing It By Ear** (32-35): Sound intensity is measured in decibels (dB). In 1979, D.B. Fry published a reference scale relating decibel increments to the average intensities of some everyday sounds.

**Forgiveness** (59): In physics, "forgiveness" is a collective term for impact resistance, fracture toughness, fatigue-crack growth rate, etc.